MILTOS SAHTOURIS

SELECTED POEMS

SELECTED POEMS

SACHEM PRESS Old Chatham, New York

MILTOS SAHTOURIS

Translated from the Greek, and with
an introduction, by Kimon Friar

ACKNOWLEDGMENTS

Some of these poems have appeared in the periodicals *Athene, The Charioteer, The Chicago Review, Dream Helmet, The Falcon, Jazz, Kayak, Linguis, Poetry* (Chicago), *Poetry: Wales* and *Shenandoah,* and in the anthologies *Modern European Poetry* (Bantam Books, 1966) and *The Unicorn and the Garden* (The Word Works, Inc., 1978). Acknowledgment is also made for the poems and the Introduction (of which the Introduction to this book is an expanded version) included in Míltos Sahtoúris, *With Face to the Wall* (The Charioteer Press, 1968; revised and expanded edition, 1980).

Published by Sachem Press, P.O. Box 9, Old Chatham, NY 12136

Printed in the United States of America

Library of Congress Cataloging in Publication Data

Sachtourēs, Miltos, 1919-
  Selected poems.

  I. Friar, Kimon. II. Title.
PA5610.S18A24   889'.134   81-21374
ISBN 0-937584-03-7   AACR2
ISBN 0-937584-04-5 (pbk.)

CONTENTS

INTRODUCTION

Míltos (Miltiades) Sahtoúris was born in Athens on July 29, 1919, but regards as his place of origin the illustrious island of Hýdra where his great, great grandfather insured his place in the history of his country as one of her admirals during the Greek War of Independence. His father's profession as Legal Counsel of the State necessitated a move soon after the infant's birth to Thessaloníki, then to Náfplion, and finally and permanently to Athens again when the boy was five years old. Between the ages of twelve and twenty he spent every summer on the family's estate in the Pelopponesos opposite Hýdra, exploring and hunting throughout the countryside. Although in his early years he endured the formal training and routine observances of Athenian youth, and even, according to his father's wishes, completed his studies in law at the University of Athens, he quit the university two years after his father's death in 1939 without troubling to take his degree and symbolically burned all his books.

A tall, burly man of athletic build but with eyes agitated by the pale cast of thought (somewhat reminiscent of the stature and sensitivity of Theodore Roethke), he saluted the heroism and enterprises of his stalwart ancestors, then resolutely turned his back on all the world of affairs, public studies, business and social amenities. Living on an extremely small income, especially since 1955 when his mother died after a lingering and expensive illness, he disappeared into an inner world of his own, one of remarkable consistency. "After my mother died," he said, "I began slowly to strip myself naked of many things, both inner and outer. Slowly my vision became more penetrating and my hearing sharper, so that I saw and heard better what it was that things had been revealing to me *behind* their facades." He has never visited abroad, and even within the boundaries of Greece has traveled little, living exclusively in one city. Even in Athens, which he rarely leaves, he confines himself, almost as narrowly and contentedly as Emily Dickinson before him, to his immediate neighborhood and a small group of friends and relatives. His soul, also, has selected her own Divine Majority and shut the valves of her attention like stone. Since 1964 he has been living in an extremely small apartment consisting of one narrow bed-sitting room, a tiny bathroom, and a kitchen as small as a closet. On his walls are photographs of Kafka, Rilke and Dylan Thomas; two small student's bookcases contain the only books he cares to have about him; the rest are packed away in suitcases. He has no television set, rarely listens to the radio except to follow the news and the soccer scores, and seldom goes to the movies, concerts or theater.

His poems come to him in sudden, unexpected flashes, sometimes in sleep or dream, sometimes when walking down the street or riding on a bus or streetcar, or during long afternoons when he sits for hours in some coffeehouse or confectionary store in his neighborhood, watching the world go by. Then come many months of polishing and rewriting, of cutting to the bone. Except for some translations into Greek from the French from time to time for various encyclopedias, he has never held a job or a position of any sort, but has devoted himself exclusively to his poetry. Even when seeming idle or chatting of inconsequential matters, he has rarely ceased to live from within the center of his being as a poet, and has never thought of poetry as a profession, but as a mission. In a sense his poems are the continuous biographical notations of his subconscious. "Instinctive poets like myself," he once wrote me, "do not well know what they are writing about. From what I consciously know of my poetry, I would say it is lyrical with a dramatic texture. The themes are usually about pain—pain for humanity, for things, for the difficulties of our dramatic times, and particularly about love, which is always so alive, so difficult, and so near death."

As a student in grade school and high school, he had never much cared about modern Greek literature. Poetry in particular irritated him, the rhymes especially; the only poets for whom he felt some sympathy were Caváfis and Kariotákis. During his first two years at the university he haphazardly wrote two or three short stories, and in 1941 published a small volume of verse, *The Music of the Islands*, under the pseudonym Miltos Hrisánthis, but which he has since rejected as juvenalia, not to be admitted into the corpus of his works. But suddenly, in 1944, to his great surprise, he felt impelled to write poetry of a kind rather advanced and radical for his day, a poetry rather surrealist, although he had not as yet read the surrealists. Later he took for mentors the Greek surrealist poets Nikos Engonópoulos and Andréas Emberícos, and the early Odysseus Elýtis and found in surrealism a climate natively his own which for the first time gave him a method and a technique by which to express the horror and absurdity of the world about him. "My point of departure," he once wrote me, "was surrealism, and although many still think of me as a surrealist, I believe my poetry has long ceased to be of this nature entirely." "Surrealism," he wrote later, "freed me from many things. It freed me, first of all, from an austere paternal education and from a narrow family tradition. As a technique, it taught me to listen to what's genuine in poetry and to use all words fearlessly."

9

From his private country Sahtoúris sends us the image-laden and blood-splattered reports of an explorer from what seems at first to be another planet. At times they read like the reports of a missionary, a doctor, a diagnostician, an astronaut, a savior, and at times like the cryptic declarations of a Cumaean Sybil, the mad but prophetic utterances of a Cassandra. It is from these, arranged in chronological order, that I have chosen, icon after icon, the existentially absurd, strange, obsessed, neurotic, nightmarish, yet nostalgic and incantatory poems of Míltos Sahtoúris, and which, we realize, reflect our own world like the underwater traceries of our most familiar objects: *The Forgotten Woman*, 1945; *Ballads*, 1948; *With Face to the Wall*, 1952; *When I Speak to You*. 1956; *The Phantoms or Joy in the Other Street*, 1958; *The Stroll*, 1960; *The Stigmata*, 1962; *The Seal or The Eighth Moon*, 1964; *The Vessel*, 1971; *Poems, 1945-1971;* and *Color Wounds*, 1980. He won First Prize in an international contest for young poets sponsored by the Italian Radio and Television System in 1956; was granted the Second State Prize in Greece for 1962; shared the Third State Prize for 1964; and was given a Ford Foundation Grant in 1972. His poems have been translated into English, German, French, Italian, Spanish, Polish, Syrian, Bulgarian, and Serbian.

Perhaps the title of his third book best describes the stance and perspective Míltos Sahtoúris has taken: *With Face to the Wall*. His rigidity in that position is suggestive of many causes and many effects. It is that of a small child who has been placed in a corner facing a wall by parent or teacher. He stands there, not quite understanding why he is being punished, but beginning to feel, as time lapses into time, that he must indeed have been guilty of some great sin, some unspeakable crime. The only recourse of the child is to shut his eyes tight and fly off into a world of his own fantastic compensation. It is also a position taken on his own volition by a man in early youth who deliberately turns his back on the world that he may gaze into it more piercingly. The world on which he now stares with a third, inner eye, is that which separates lover from lover, husband from wife, friend from friend, nation from nation, no matter of what material it is composed: iron, bamboo, silk, stone, invisible glass, or yielding air. It is at once barrier and barricade, stronghold and iron cage, prison and asylum wall. It is the Wailing Wall where every minority group—and whose numbers are more depleted than those of the true poets?—bewails its fate and thus the fate of all individuals and of all nations. And it is finally that wall in Greece during the German-Italian Occupation of the early 1940s against which—as against all similar walls throughout the world—men, women and children, poets among them (as in Spain),

10

were ruthlessly propped up as hostages and shot down by rifle or machinegun fire. It is a nightmare world of Hitler and Hiroshima that makes the distorted and dislocated images of Sahtoúris seem but pale depictions of actual events. He belongs to the postwar generation of poets who had seen the whitewashed walls of Greece suddenly splattered red, and all his poetry has been colored by this terror, recorded in such poems as "Nightmare," "He Is Not Oedipus," or "Death." History is forever brutally repeating itself: Aegisthus and Orestes become equated with Kostas and Alexis, Oedipus with Elias the grocer, the descent of the Virgin Mary with the ascent of Achilles' horses, hand grenades with bitter oranges. As in *Macbeth*, one word, on a background of black and white, colors most of his poetry: blood.

When asked during an interview if he believes that poets express the problems of their times, Sahtoúris answered, "Yes, necessarily. It has been truly said that if only poems were to be saved after a general catastrophe, we should be able to reconstruct from poems alone the entire history of humanity." Although he does not espouse any political party or write "committed" poetry, his penetrating vision of the world within and without himself is in the deepest sense "committed" since he feels himself to be a sensitive receiver in the very center of the vortex. He has not documented his themes, for instance, like Yánnis Rítsos, Manólis Anagnostákis, or Tákis Sinópoulos, but as the poet and critic Yánnis Dállas[1] has written, he has *absorbed* his times, much, I might add, as a saint or an innocent or a child. And yet, all his poems are at heart neither cruel nor basically pessimistic, but are rather spells, incantations and exorcisms against evil in the world.

It would be correct to say that Sahtoúris did not at first choose of his own free will to stand with his face to the wall. Like most of us during the past two generations, he was placed there first by parents, priest, or teacher for punishment, or out of original sin; then by the enemy, and finally by some Kafkaesque tribunal of the universe, unknown and mysterious. It was only later that he recognized his personal wounds to be the stigmata of the entire world's guilt. Like Maria, in the poem by that name, when everyone began to speak to him unbearably, as through a medium, he took refuge by beginning to fly in imagination round and round a room that was both prison and escape, for, as he writes in "The Saviour," "every room is an open wound." He is obsessed with disease, and his creatures are as stigmatized as Grünewald's Christ and demons in the Isenheim Altarpiece. "And if I should find the pharmacy closed," he cries out, "and if I should find the pharmacist dead/and if I should find my naked heart in the pharmacy

[1] Yánnis Dállas, *Introduction to the Poetry of Míltos Sahtoúris.* Athens: Kédhros, 1979. [In Greek.]

window?" In his early verses image follows image without much logical intent, as in the naturally surrealist world of childhood, evoking in their totality worlds of alienation, agony, lost innocence, love betrayed, fear, anxiety, guilt. It would be futile in many of these poems, and in the whole of Sahtoúris' work, to attempt any thorough logical deduction or sequential exegesis. "My poetry is many things," he once wrote me, "which elude me and which I do not understand. And if I did understand, I would not wish to reveal it."

The mature poet opened his eyes and gazed intently on the mottled wall before him. From its patterns formed by rain, mold, decay, moss, blood, and sunstains, and from remembrance of the world behind him, he constructed a mirror-world of his own. "Poetry, without my being aware of it," Sahtoúris told me, "was like a mirror of my inner self, and behold, I held in my hands another mirror in which everything I saw was reflected. I shattered both mirrors, and from the splintered crystals built my own Orpheus-mirror in which true poetry stands revealed, my own life." A wall gazed on so intently, so persistently, so obsessively does indeed become a reflective image, a hallucination, a water-mirror into which Narcissus may drown, or a shield-mirror where Perseus may slay the monster Medusa of form by subtle indirection. In this world of inverted images, girls fall on their backs and spit on their dreams, a dog drinks up his tears on the ground, lovers carve trees on their hearts, plates break as soon as they are touched, kisses open and close on the floor, moons are knifed, a kneeling horse eats up floorboards, saints run in the streets, and bats fly like sorrowful gospels.

Like most poets who in childhood fled into a world fantastically yet naturally their own, Sahtoúris later in youth grasped gratefully at the techniques of surrealism to depict a world of images that had an irrational logic of its own. But when he tried to pierce through his enclosures and into the world beyond and behind, his poems became increasingly lyrical and dramatic. Without abandoning the dislocated imagery of surrealism, which coincides with his natural view of the world, he found that his images began to convey an immediately apprehensible picturization of the world's own dislocations. Neither metaphor, simile, symbolism or allegory play a central role in his poetry. Instead, images are juxtaposed against one another in such a way that they do not blur into each other or lose their clean autonomous outlines but, on the contrary, create a state of tension between them. The clash of their absurd juxtapositions arouses few reverberations but instead creates an intense translucency through which we glimpse signals of meaning when the eye shifts and lays one transparent tracery over another until the composite yet clear imagery often takes on a mystery as obscure to the poet as it is to us. Everything is cleanly visualized, luminous, sharp in outline, yet everything is at the same time a hallucinatory revelation. The full burden of Sahtoúris' vision is contained almost entirely in his images.

His poems are almost all very short, written in unrhymed free verse (with very few exceptions), in brief declarative or interrogative sentences with the simplest diction and syntax. They reveal at times a strangely silent world, like that of Chirico or Magritte, like that of old cinematic films, like that of Picasso's "Guernica," and although there is often dialogue or a sudden cry of agony—a dog or a dove or a virgin howls—we look into mouths that are gaping wounds without sound. But they are, as the title of his last book emphatically states, *Color Wounds.* One of his earliest memories is that of playing by himself in the prismatic reflections cast on the floor by the sun shining through a pane of many-colored glass set in the door of his parents' home in Náfplion. Checkered like a harlequin on that chromatic ground, he played theater, creating scene after scene, as he was later to do in his poems. It has been calculated that in his *Poems, 1945-1971,* there are references to 526 colors in 234 pages,[2] over two colors to a page. Those that predominate are black (105) red (82) and white (56), creating a dramatically vivid background on which are splattered green (23), gold (13), azure (12), yellow (11), and a dwindling array of other hues. "I shall cast colors everywhere," he declares in "The Nobleman," and does so with a lavish hand. His colors, however, as in Chagall, do not depict nature realistically but invoke states of soul. The daydream world of Chagall becomes the nightmare world of Sahtoúris: his singing or floating heads, flying girls, lovers hanging from trees, hearts nesting in high mountains, dead children or corpses ascending into the sky mingle darkly with Chagall's airborne lovers with their yellow bodies, his winged goats or fishes, his floating or flying horses, carts, sleighs, caps, fish, madonnas, children, or bearded peddlers. Both live in an inverted world of heads, girls, pigeons or monsters floating upside-down. Chagall creates a world of blue horses, green cocks, goats or faces, bearded children or bird-headed men, roosters playing violins; and Sahtoúris creates an analogous color-wounded world of men-pigeons, butterfly- or sky-dogs where doves, lambs and moons howl, donkeys and roosters sing, birds talk, count, or fall in love, dogs and hares groan or weep, and fishes write, study, or burn. Both live in

---

[2]See D.N. Maronítis, *Míltos Sahtoúris: Men—Colors—Animals—Machines.* Athens: Gnósi, 1980. [In Greek.] In this book, the statistics listed are 526 colors in 265 pages. True, *Poems, 1945-1971* does have a total of 165 pages, but 31 of these are devoid of poems, given over to titles, dedications, etc. The proportion of colors to a page, nevertheless, though slightly greater, remains about the same; 2½ colors to a page. I have taken their count of colors on faith.

13

an absurd world accompanied by a humanity and a bestiary all their own floating in a metamorphosis of color. Hieronymus Bosch is their intermediary.

It is in this world of alienation that Sahtoúris lives, loves, and suffers. When his friends stray into another room, it is as though he has lost them forever. Love is the most shattering experience of all, filled with erotic obsessions, forever found and forever lost, a heavy sickness: lovers are puppets pushed, not pulled by strings. "My poetry is fundamentally erotic," Sahtoúris once wrote me. "It is composed of two bodies that embrace until suddenly they discover that their faces are black and besmirched with blood."

Yet no man, no poet, pushed to such extremity, has not been impelled there by an inordinate love of the world, of all animate and inanimate things. Sahtoúris' agony is not that of illusion but of disillusion, horror at the brutality of a world a thousand-fold more surrealist than his own. Occasionally, therefore, he celebrates what must have been the pristine innocence of childhood and the world, what man and the world may one day still hopefully become. His belief is that poetry, no matter how shattering, may transform tragedy by shaping it into the ordered beauty of image and cadence. He sprinkles ugliness with beauty, casts a rainbow spray of colors among his gaping images, wants every spring to be judged by its own gladness, nails us to the pavement that we may admire the celestial advertisement, transforms mundane reality into cinematic art that defies death until one day, he declares, we may "pass through the black burning hole of the sun." In "The Poet," Sahtoúris has written his own epitaph: a white bird shall recite his verses in a frightening darkness, but where, as in "Threnody," the color of birds will sing, butterflies will strike back at knives, and the night shall become as beautiful as day.

KIMON FRIAR
Athens, and the Villa Giornata, Ekáli.

14

MILTOS SAHTOURIS

SELECTED POEMS

The Difficult Sunday

Since morning I've been looking upward at a better bird
since morning I've been rejoicing at a snake coiled around my neck

Broken water glasses on the rug
crimson flowers the cheeks of the prophetess
when she lifts the dress of fate
something will grow out of this joy
a new tree without flowers
or an innocent new eyelash
or an adored word
that has not kissed forgetfulness on the mouth

Outside the bells are clamoring
outside unimaginable friends are waiting for me
they lift a dawn high and twirl it round
what weariness what weariness
yellow dress—an eagle embroidered—
green parrot—I close my eyes—it shrieks
always always always
the orchestra plays counterfeit tunes
what suffering eyes what women
what loves what voices what loves
friend love blood friend
friend give me your hand what cold

It was freezing
I no longer know the hour when they all died
and I remained with an amputated friend
and with a blooded branch for company

Beauty

He sprinkled ugliness with beauty
he took a guitar
and walked along a riverbank
singing

He lost his voice
the delirious lady stole it
who cut off her head in the crimson waters
and the poor man no longer has a voice to sing with
and the river rolls
the tranquil head with its eyelashes closed

Singing

The Dream

Notre voyage à nous est entièrement
imaginaire. Voilà sa force.
    —L.F. Céline

The everliving dream
caresses its white hair

Boys undress in the light
throw the ball and shout in triumph
a Frankish priest points with his finger at Lycabbétos
a naked boy smiles at the girls
they grow tall in their branches they shout
he is crippled he is crippled
afterwards they plunge in shame in the red water

Young women undress in the shadow
in the endless harbor frightened
a surgeon on the balcony opens and closes his lancets
tired stevedores lie in wait
to cut the ship's cables
to tear the unvirginal dresses to tatters
to mutiny and hang the captain
from the large mast of the sky
for women to clench their fingers
to close their eyes to sigh
to show their teeth their tongues

The voyage of joy begins

The suffering woman undressed in the dark
she swarmed up the wretched house and
stopped the futile music
she laughed in the mirror lifted her hands
painted her face with the color
of an expectation saw the sun
in her watch and then remembered:

18

"Look, the poem has come true
and the illegitimate boy and the color
make a gift of joy
and how can they photograph this place
it is a place of hypocrisy
it is a land where boys
who have lost their innocence lie in ambush
and spread out their hands to the open windows
that the sick kisses might fall
that the young short-lived orphans
might fall weeping from the windows
squeezing in their wounded hands
a tuft of white hair

From the very ancient dream"

The Saviour

I count on the fingers of my severed hands
the hours I have strayed in these rooms of the wind
I do not have other hands my beloved and the doors
do not want to close and the dogs are unyielding

With my bare feet I splash in these dirty waters
with my bare heart I search (not for myself)
for a skyblue window
how did they ever build so many rooms so many tragic books
without a crack of light
without a breath of oxygen
for the sick reader

Since every room is also an open wound
how shall I descend the crumbling stairs again
to bring through mud and wild dogs again
bandages of rose and medicines
and if I should find the pharmacy closed
and if I should find the pharmacist dead
and if I should find my naked heart in the pharmacy window

No no it is ended there is no salvation

The rooms shall remain as they are
with the wind and the reeds of the wind
with splinters of glass faces that groan
with their colorless bleeding
with porcelain hands that stretch out toward me
with unpardonable oblivion

My own *fleshy* hands forgot they had been severed
the moment I was counting up their agony

The Three Lovers

On the rain-soaked roads of evening
rises a haze of seablue light
a broad hand on each heart
and with ruinous footsteps
three lovers hand in hand go by
                    the first

Hangs his love on a tree
and prays beneath the tree at midnight
for his love to descend clinging to the leaves
for the flood of melting leaves to cease
a dog drinks up his tears on the ground
and love amidst the branches stones him
the tree howls the wind the dog
                    the second

Gave his love away to a crazy violinist
the crazy man made a song about it
the sky rains down flowers coins
the roads resound with the fatal violin
all have now learned the song of love
with bluecold puckered lips they whistle it
but only he does not know it
                    the third

Made a boat out of his love
and launched it on the three seas
he has now become a boy again
and builds castles of sand
he gathers shells pebbles
and waits for his boat for love
to return again

All three have carved a tree on their hearts
a violin played close to the ear will drive them crazy
and in the underseas the captain plays with coral

The Forgotten Woman

I

This furrow is not a furrow of blood
this ship is not a ship of storm
this wall is not a wall of sensuality
this crumb is not a crumb of holiday
this dog is not a dog of flowers
this tree is not a tree electrical
this house is not a house of hesitation

The white old woman is not an old woman about to die

They are a spoonful of sweet wine the vigor of joy
for the life of the forgotten woman

II

The forgotten woman opens her window
she opens her eyes
trucks with women dressed in black pass by below
who display their naked sex
with one-eyed drivers who blaspheme
by her Christ and her Virgin Mary
the women in black wish her evil
and let them throw carnations at her steeped in blood
from the effervescence of their sensual gardens
from the evaporation of gasoline in a cloud of smoke
the drivers
tear through the cloud and call her prostitute
but she is a Dolorous Virgin
with her beloved amid the icons
precisely as time has preserved him
with the candles of all the betrayed
who marched to death between the daisies and the camomile
with beldames servants and mountain stars
with swords that slashed through throats and palm trees

III

The forgotten woman stretches out her white hand
takes however a piece of colored glass and sings
"I call to you not from within the dream
but from among these splinters of multi-colored glasses
yet you always recede
now indeed your face frightens me truly
no matter how much I try to match these broken glasses
I can no longer face you wholly
at times I only construct your head
among a thousand other savage heads that estrange me
at times only your beloved body
among a thousand other amputated bodies
at times again only your blessed hand
among a thousand other outflung hands
that encumber my feet under my dresses
they blindfold me with their black handkerchiefs
they command me to walk and not turn back my head
to see your eyes shattering"

IV

The forgotten woman in the depths of her victorious sleep
holding an apple in her right hand caressing the sea with the
    other
suddenly unfolds her beautiful eyes
it is only a breeze the roar of a cannon
it is only the bicyclist his beloved and a bouquet of flowers
it is the clamor of the heart the smoke of minefields
it is hatred bodies that couple in rage and sink
it is a dreadful kiss on the frontiers of sensuality
where five deaths may be found sown among the poppies
it is the shadow of her lover passing by

V

Forty years later the forgotten woman shall uproot these words.
And shall I say that on this street miracles happen? No. Miracles
happen only in haunted churches. Shall I speak of the man
who became a tree and of his mouth that sprouted with flowers?
I am shy but I must speak no matter if no one believes me. The
only one who could have believed me was killed there before the
altar, a few naked boys stoned him to death. They wanted to kill a
wolf-hound they wanted to sing a song they wanted to kiss a
woman. At all events they killed him and cut him in two with a
saber. From the waist up they put him in a window as a statue.
From the waist down they taught him to walk like a toddling child.
He did not seem worthy enough to become a good statue for his
eye would not turn white. And then again his feet cut a great
many crazy capers and frightened the women who spend the night
in windows. Now from the sides of his lips two small bitter leaves
have sprouted. Extremely green. Is he a flower or a man? Is he a
man or a statue? Is he a statue or a lurking death? Forty years
later the forgotten woman shall uproot these words.

VI

The forgotten woman is the soldier who was crucified
the forgotten woman is the clock that stopped
the forgotten woman is the branch that caught fire
the forgotten woman is the needle that broke
the forgotten woman is the tomb of Christ that blossomed
the forgotten woman is the hand that aimed
the forgotten woman is the back that shuddered
the forgotten woman is the kiss that sickened
the forgotten woman is the knife that missed
the forgotten woman is the mud that dried
the forgotten woman is the fever that fell

from BALLADS (1948)

The Almond Trees

Dazzling house white and red
in what room have your almond trees blossomed
I have lived in all your corners
in the red one and the unhappy one
in the tragic white one there in the loft
your breathing has blurred my dreams
on your windowpanes a sea quivered and faded
gardens of secret chrysanthemums in your ecstasy
where I ran hunting and blood-splattered

A large net passed straight
above my head
unhappiness had iron teeth
the sun even planted other gardens on the walls
the garden of the fly the garden of the paper kite
the great garden of love
and the garden of the great fever
where all day long I wandered with my gun
with a red ribbon in my mouth
with a red ribbon in my hair
like the red corner and the unhappy one
like the tragic white corner there in the loft
I have lived in all the corners
in which ones then did your almond trees grow

The Wounded Spring

Wounded Spring stretches her flowers taut
the night bells their clamor
and the pure-white girl amid the carnations
gathers the blood drop by drop
from all the flags that ever felt pain
from the cypress trees that were slaughtered
that a deep red tower might be built
with a clock and two black clockhands
and when the clockhands cross a cloud will come
and when the clockhands cross a sword will come
the cloud will inflame the carnations
the sword will reap her body

The Dead Man in our Life, John Benjamin d'Arkózi*

To Níkos Engonópoulos

John Benjamin d'Arkózi who died—"in life"—and was re-surrected as soon as night fell slaughters his herds every evening—goats cows and many sheep—drowns all his birds empties his rivers and on the pitch-black cross he has erected in the middle of his room crucifies his beloved. Afterwards he sits before his open window smoking his pipe poor and tearful and thinks if only he too had herds of cows goats many sheep if only he had rivers with swift pellucid waters if he too could marvel at the fluttering of birds if only he too could take joy in a woman's warm breath.

*The name is imaginary. [Tr.]

Observatory

Burglars of the sun
they had never before seen a green twig
they had never touched a flaming mouth
they do not know what the color of the sky is

In darkened rooms locked up
they do not know if they will die
they lurk in ambush
with black masks and heavy telescopes
with stars in their pockets dirty with crumbs
with stones of cowards in their hands
they lurk in other planets for the light

Let them die

Let every Spring be judged by its gladness
by its color every single flower
by its caress every single hand
by its trembling every single kiss

Nightmare

Her name was *Seashore* and *Sunday*. She had black eyes black hair black garments black petticoats and a pure black horse. But they called her *Seashore* and *Sunday*. Her house was on an island and it was full of pistols crimson robes flags netted stars machine guns diving helmets hooks chests with dreams and chests with bullets island dresses lamps with colored glasses colored handkerchiefs and an old rusted cannon. As night fell she would light a lantern in the window. It would flare up—go out flare up—go out and immediately a wretched boat would anchor by the side of the iron door of the house and one by one five men would glide into the house. In a little while from a small secret door covered with cactus the First Man emerged dead. The Second with his face splattered with blood held a very beautiful infant tightly in his arms. The Third also splattered with blood held an automatic rifle tightly in his arms. The Fourth dragged himself along wrapped from top to toe in a heavy dark green material. The Fifth was dead also. But the most wonderfully dead person was the girl in her pure white dress lying in the middle of the room by the side of her slain black horse she also inundated with blood her hands crossed high on her breasts with a smile and a green twig in her mouth while the five Germans weak before her saluted at attention.

The Gifts

Today I wore a
warm red blood
today people love me
a woman smiled at me
a girl gave me a seashell
a boy gave me a hammer

Today I kneel on the sidewalk
and nail the naked white feet of the passersby
to the pavement tiles
they are all in tears
but no one is frightened
all remain in the places to which I had come in time
they are all in tears
but they gaze at the celestial advertisements
at a beggar who sells hot cross buns
in the sky

Two men whisper
what is he doing is he nailing our hearts?

Yes he is nailing our hearts

Well then he is a poet

Death

No one killed this particular man
he was not the harbor watchman
he was not a warrior in battle
in trains he would bring animals in iron cages
and his heart nested on the high mountains
some time or other his blood will speak
and then dark black birds will smother the clouds
bearded black winds will encircle the fields
pear trees will sing his history
in the house of flame with the wild animals
the cups of death upon the table
the sunless curtains the lamp and cold words
lamp and cold kisses without love
with the wanton girls of silence
who every evening would close the windows
who every evening would crucify sleep
who every evening would tear up and eat their dresses
they would fall on their backs and spit on their dreams

Deep Mine

I write you filled with fear from a nocturnal arcade
lit by a lamp as small as a thimble
a wagon carefully passes above me
it gropes its distances so as not to hit me
but sometimes I pretend to be sleeping sometimes
to be darning a pair of old stockings
because all things about me have strangely grown old

At home
yesterday
as I opened the wardrobe it vanished it turned
to dust together with all its clothing
the plates break as soon as they're touched
I'm afraid and have hidden the knives and forks
my hair has become somewhat like cotton batting
my mouth has turned white and hurts me
my hands are stone
my feet are wooden
three small children wander about me crying
I don't know how this happened and they call me *mother*

I wanted to write you of our old happiness
but I have forgotten how to write of happy things

R e m e m b e r m e

The Sky

Birds, black arrows of difficult sorrow
it is not easy for you to love the sky
you have learned well to say it is blue
do you know its caves its forests its rocks?
As you are passing thus like winged whistles
you tear your flesh on its windowpanes
your downy feathers are glued to its heart

And when night comes fearfully from the trees
you look at the sky's white handkerchief the moon
at the naked virgin who howls in its lap
at the mouth of the old lady with its rotted teeth
at the stars with swords and golden strings
at its lightning its thunder its rain
at the distant sensuality of its galaxy

Peter

Again what cannibalism this Spring
flowers have greedily swallowed the honeybees
hawks have eaten the entrails of birds
the rose has remained utterly alone
and the violet has become transformed into a funeral

I have no other flowers to bring you
but one day I will become the great gardener
I shall plant, I shall prune, I shall water
I shall build my house on a cloud
I shall light my dreams with the sun

Today I am still a pilot
also guilty for the mud the lemon peels
the tin cans in the harbor waters
I drive the siren insane I sow my blood
I wear stone glasses and I am called Peter

The Door

To Yórgos Líkos

The door you opened with such passion
opened toward Death
and three flowers can't cover him
and the sugary cheeks of the girl
behind the door
can't exorcise him
behind the door the girl undresses in the wind
the cypress trees whisper a prayer of snow
the gloomy north wind howls and bends the branches
the woodsmen have vanished in the sea
pale fishing boats have lowered their flags
bugles in the sea-depths have trumpeted the end
while in the harbor all come out for a Sunday stroll
women in black drag their little boys behind them
blacksmiths torture their ill-fated horses
savage barrel-organs knife their tambourines
children sell lollipops red as snow
ships and birds whistle and leave
masts open a road between the stars
the door you opened with care
has a thousand other doors behind it
behind each door there is a cry
behind each door a girl stands upright

The Battle

You stretched you always stretched out your hands
on the balconies you helped the sick
to descend
with their large eyes their thin legs their flowers
while all around them from the dark windows
t h e y   w e r e   a l l   s h o o t i n g

You stretched you always stretched out your stride
wherever there were high mountains or big roads
big roads with fires and revolvers
with a poor man who was giving away the lives of saints
with a gypsy woman who wanted an egg passionately
to make creation within it sigh

You stretched you always stretched out your stride
and in the rain the hanged man
stood at Attention
with his golden stripes his violin his handkerchief
with ten clouds of mud in his heart
and from the mud small children took
and built ten dream cities

You stretched you always stretched out your hands
and the sick now had vanished in the streets below
with their large eyes their thin legs their songs
while all around them from the dark windows
t h e y   w e r e   a l l   s h o o t i n g

The Brigand

The thud of stars on high
and the green grass below
and an electric iron rooster
emits flame
the clock stops in the clouds
at the door the brigand
the panther
with the long lance
with the long black hair
like a woman of ancient times
with a blood-stained egg in her hand
around him the railings the jasmine
the shadow of the moon
the shadow of teeth in blood
the mud
the cross
the clock counts
the clock is not living
and her voice
is heard darkly
her heart boils
like old wine forgotten
down deep
forty stairs
the clock counts
forty
forty days
and forty years
the clock is not living

Lazarus

"Today all things are new
the year gifts hopes
and only my heart
is beaten by ancient hurricanes"

Rain in the arcades rain
hail in automobiles
with frozen feet
see how the guard is watching you
photographs deaths hopes

Coals in the heart of Lazarus

Rise from your bed Lazarus
they are giving you a distant place
a meadow tender with anemones
a dreadful meadow
Rise from your bed Lazarus
factory owner Lazarus evil Lazarus
become a river of spring Lazarus
become an earring become a whirlwind
love life

"Today all things are new
see how the guard is watching you
photographs deaths hopes
and only my heart
is beaten by ancient hurricanes"

The Factory

Factory factory
of night and fire
with large suns made of roses
fire ladders
poplar trees—ghosts with red leaves
despairing birds tied with harsh
white string
frightful toys

The bride smiles
with soiled arm
with cracked hand
with painted nails
the ship anchored by the pierside
and further down the storm
and further down the drowned man

He She

The tired horses by the rain's side
thirst
and further beyond thirst

The Poet

Kept his gardens hidden in his mouth
that burned and filled the land with smoke

Factory factory
fright and flame

Sometimes the Women

Sometimes a bird comes out of a cloud
it passes over the houses and descends into the city
once it remained for years imprisoned in the moon
and this is why it is very bitter very brilliant
with only one large beautiful woman's eye

Out of the cloud it descends in the rain
it passes like a phantom over the houses
in the streets they call it bird bird of the rain
it doesn't remain anywhere because if it should stop
a thousand scattered fingers will point at it
because it is a cruel bird dyed in blood
that descends into the city ferociously with the rain
and has one very beautiful woman's eye

This is why women are alarmed when they see it
but some hide it in their mirrors
some hide it in deep drawers
and some deep in their bodies
and so it cannot be seen
it cannot be seen by the men who caress them at night
nor in the morning when the women dress before the mirror
they cannot see it
because it is a bird very bitter very beautiful
very frightened

He Is Not Oedipus

A huge sky filled with swallows
enormous halls doric columns
the hungry ghosts
sitting in chairs in corners
weeping
the rooms with dead birds
Aegisthus the fishing net Kostas
Kostas the fisherman the afflicted
a room filled with tulles of many colors fluttering
    in the wind
bitter-oranges break the windowpanes
and enter
Kostas killed
Orestes killed
Alexis killed
break the chains on the windows
and enter
Kostas Orestes Alexis
others return to the streets from the fiesta
with lights with flags with trees
they call on Maria to come down
they call on Maria to come down from Heaven
the horses of Achilles fly in the heavens
rockets attend their flight
the sun rolls down from hill to hill
and the moon is a green lantern
filled with alcohol
then silence falls like night on the streets
and the blind man comes out with his cane
children follow him on tiptoe
he is not Oedipus
he is Elias from the vegetable market
he plays an exhausting and fatal flute
he is dead Elias from the vegetable market

Pasiphae

The frozen hands
search the clouds
find the windmill
in the clouds
turning without wings
find the headless ghost
of the chimney
find the cross
of the savage threat
the perforated
jar of rain
they also find
the spring moon
extinguished
smoking
with lilac flowers
all about it
the frozen hands
seize Ariadne's
thread
and then find
the wooden cow
of the queen
smashed
into little pieces
and in the clouds
they even find
how shall I say it

her very eyes

savage insane
and thirsty

like lightning flashes

On the Nature of the Beast

Do not go away beast
beast with the iron teeth
I shall build you a wooden house
I shall give you an earthen jug
I shall also give you a spear
I shall give you more blood to play with

I shall bring you to other harbors
to see how ships devour their anchors
how masts break in two
and how flags are suddenly painted black

I shall find for you the same girl again
trembling at night bound in the dark
I shall find for you the broken balcony again
and the sky-dog
that kept the rain in the well

I shall find for you the same soldiers again
he who vanished three years ago
with a hole above his eyes
and he who knocks on doors at night
with amputated hand

I shall find for you the rotten apple again

Do not go away beast
beast with the iron teeth

Experiments for the Repetition of Night

My friends are leaving
they have come to say goodbye

I shall never see my friends again

one of them is leaving for the adjacent room
his face has turned black
he has worn a dark green material
night has fallen
he no longer speaks

the other is leaving for the other room
to find the pins
first however he hid himself behind the curtains
he became frightened
afterwards he climbed on the window
to sleep

the other took off his shoes
with trembling hands
he took the warm
statue
into the bedroom
but doesn't know how to make it stand upright

my friends have gone far away

I shall not see my friends
again

The Crossing

When I was going up the streets
and the moon burned my hands
the owl, the baker's daughter, would wake up
then I would go out and call the Night

When I was going down the river
her secret wounded my chest
the tanner had nowhere to sleep
then I would go out and call the Night

When I was going up the stairs
and the quails got tangled in my feet
and dragged the man by the hair
then I would go out and call the Night

When I was going down the stairs
and they waited there for me to tell them
and roses sprouted in the kitchen sink
then I would go out and call the Night

And when I would take to the streets again
and the irons rose out of the ground
and the thank you writhed in the blood
then I would go out and call the Night

The Scene

On the table they had set
a head of clay
they had decorated their walls
with flowers
on the bed they had cut out of paper
two erotic bodies
on the floor snakes slithered
and butterflies
a huge dog kept guard
in the corner

Strings stretched across the room
from all sides
it would be imprudent for anyone
to pull them
one of the strings tugged at the bodies
to make love

The unhappiness outside
clawed the doors

The Sheep

O head of mine filled with dream
hands of mine filled with mud

Well should I also sing of the rain
when Pontius Pilate walked in the streets
no one recognized his face
in the darkness in the desert next to the cables
when Jesus was multiplying the fishes
one man leant on a hedge
another on a blind bridge
another on a ruined house
when Jesus was multiplying the fishes
and the sea was casting up on land
her wild white sheep
Pontius Pilate walked in the streets
no one however recognized his joy
Pontius Pilate the first river mate
with the cage his hungry birds
the garden his lost flowers
the two embraced on the hill
the two sighed in the arcade
the two swooned under the cypress tree
when the sea once more gathered
her wild white sheep
and put them to sleep in her bitter arms

Saturday

The dead two steps away from us
are resting
or sit quietly
on the stairs
with a bloody broom in their hands
but the living
have certain monstrous heads
full of petroleum
and their hands are smeared
with fat
they build boats out of black paper
they leave
one by one
and without sun
for the black sky

Nostalgia Returns

The woman undressed and lay on the bed
a kiss opened and closed on the floor
savage shapes with knives began to appear on the ceiling
hung on a wall, a bird choked and vanished
a candle leant and fell from its holder
weeping was heard outside and the clatter of feet

The windows opened a hand entered
afterward the moon entered
embraced the woman and they slept together

All night long a voice was heard:

T h e   d a y s   p a s s
t h e   s n o w   r e m a i n s

The Clouds

The clouds left
one by one
but in their place
other clouds came
more savage
more frantic
more fearful

I am said to be good
by good men
who do not know me
the way dogs know me
the way eagles
know me
or ants

Desolate
in the wet streets
with the raincoats of strangers
with tortured hands
trumpets
ghosts
and encircling threats

I Greet You

The Telephone

We telephone
for a dead man
where can we find him?
—His name?
they reply
—He has no name
he is dead
we search
the drawers
—They have hidden him
—They have chased him out
They have saved him
we can't find him
he is dead
they tell us run
in the rain
to find him
we run
and do not find him
I telephone
and they tell me He has gone
they must be lying
I see HER
with my large eye
the crimson one
Let's go elsewhere
to wander about
and to ask
—They don't know her
—They don't know his name
—They've forgotten him
I telephone
they tell me: No
—They don't know who I am
—They don't know my name
They've forgotten me

I am dead

The Carnival

This carnival took place far away in another world
the small hobbyhorse wandered in the desolate streets
where not a soul was breathing
dead children were continually rising into the sky
they would descend for a moment
to get the paper kites they had forgotten
snow fell like glass confetti
and wounded every heart
a kneeling woman
turned up her eyes as though she were dead
only troops of soldiers passed by one-two
one-two with frozen teeth

At night the moon came out
a carnival moon
filled with hate
they bound it and cast it into the sea
knifed

This carnival took place far away in another world

The Metamorphosis

One day I shall awaken
as a star
as you foretold
I shall wash the blood
from my hands
and shall cast off the nails
from my chest
I shall no longer fear thunder
I shall not fear the slain
rooster
one day I shall awaken
as a star
as you foretold
then
you will be a bird
perhaps you will be *a peacock*
I
shall have been proved innocent

from WHEN I SPEAK TO YOU (1956)

We Have Sprouted

To T.I. Roússos

We have sprouted again like wild flowers this spring
wild cherry and wild azure
but they die
we grow like statues
wild warm flowers this spring
we stretch out our hands and shout
but the reply
comes after many years
and from a great distance
like a chained ghost

and like a heavy empty ship

Eros Slipped

Eros slipped
between my fingers
and fell
into a glass filled with blood
rolled on a darkened
mirror
on which a frightful rain
fell
he vanished in a forest
filled
with shadows
songs
birds

The Orange Tree

I

What a wretched winter, my God! What a wretched winter! An
orange-colored petticoat is hanging, a rose-colored dust rag
and it is raining. An old man is looking through the windowpane.
A dry tree, a light shining the color of orange. A tree with
oranges further on. And the girl turned upside down and the
cup broken and everyone, my God, weeping weeping weeping
And then money money a great deal of money
What a wretched winter, my God! What a wretched winter, my God!
What a wretched winter

II

It is raining as in the previous poem *The Orange Tree*
A woman with a mirror and some wires is trying to hold
the years. But the years leave
the wires enter deeply into her cheeks
tear them and blood flows
as a savage hand with a piece of chalk comes and goes
and paints her hair white

The Dove

The dove was to pass this way
they had lit torches everywhere in the streets
other men kept guard by rows of trees
children held small flags in their hands
the hours passed and it began to rain
afterwards all the sky darkened
a lightning flash whispered something fearfully
and the outcry opened in the mouth of man

then the white dove with savage teeth
howled like a dog in the night

The Voyage

Don't move! the photographer shouted
but the ship had already set out
a large white ship filled with sick birds
and the birdkeeper on a terrace watched them through binoculars
as they were leaving together with the white clouds
that were also leaving

If we enter the hotel opposite they'll see us
they'll say: They've entered the hotel *Hope*

"Are you going on a trip?" the colonel asked
"No" I answered "I'm a doctor"
"I've just examined those sick birds who left
see there's even one who's escaped me"
It had crossed over to the shop opposite

"These are the last things I shall buy
with Greek money" said the sick bird
Then it opened its wings and flew into the sky

I Am Not a Tree

I am not a tree
I am not a bird
I am not a cloud
the dream has rotted in my blood
the dream has rotted in my bones
once in a dream I slew a girl
by the side of a cypress tree
now I recline beneath it
on a cloth stretched tight

I had loves
I had battles
and I lurked in corners
my nails have grown long
my lips have swollen
my face has grown black
I am not a tree
I am not a bird
I am not a cloud

The Martyrdom

The moon dripped with fragrance
dogs with white flowers on their heads
passed in the road ecstatic
the road below shone of crystal
and inside appeared
the hammers and the knives

In my hands I broke the crystal

And then I saw the red cloud
growing larger inflaming my heart
and the other one as grey as smoke
emptying out of me
and fleeing

Maria

Maria was pensively
taking off her stockings

Voices of other people
rose out of her body
that of a soldier who spoke like a bird
that of a sick man who had died from sheep pains
and the weeping of a small niece of Maria's
who in these past few days had just been born

Maria wept and wept
then Maria laughed
she spread out her hands at night
and remained with her legs open

Afterwards her eyes darkened
black black opaque they darkened

The radio played
Maria wept
Maria wept
The radio played

Then Maria
slowly slowly opened her arms
and began to fly
round and round the room

History

When the rusty door opened like a stage curtain
it creaked
like a rotted ship in an evil harbor
the face of the girl appeared deluded
in the fragrance of fire and smoke
her voice
like the dark hall of a movie house
emerged deluded
and I
a shirt hanging in the air
amid ruin
and preparing to fly

the girl
a living flower
a burning flower
a beautiful beast
her mouth turned upside down
her eyes
her eyebrows
a beautiful beast
that chimed
like a magical clock
on this magical evening

the night at last
advanced
the girl shattered in the mirror

afterward
her face
my face
appeared again
enormously
distorted
savagely drenched in blood

like a movie house

My Brothers

My brothers who disappeared down here on earth
are the stars that now light up one by one in the sky

and there's the eldest
with a black spring tie
who got lost in blindblack caves
as he rolled playing
on red anemones
he slipped
into the blood-stained mouth of the wild beast

and then my other brother who was burned
would sell yellow fireworks
he would sell and set yellow fireworks ablaze
— When we light — he would say — a fire
we shall chase the ghosts from the gardens
the ghosts shall cease polluting the gardens
— When we set — he would say — yellow fireworks ablaze
one day the sky will flame up in blue

and then the third and youngest
who would say he was a bat
this is why he loved the moons
and the moons one night encircled him
stuck around him and closed him in
stuck around him and choked him
the moons around him dissolved him

my brothers who disappeared down here on earth
are the stars that now light up one by one in the sky

The Temptation

Behind the old women dressed in black
behind their backs
is the white bed
and on it the apple utterly alone
just as before the apple
the white flower was utterly alone
they tore it with knives with scissors
they watered it with blood
and now on the bed
a rotted apple lies

This is why the angel sits by the edge of the bed
behind the old women dressed in black
behind their backs
he opens his white wings
and stretches his hand toward the apple

The Crazy Hare

It roamed the streets the crazy hare
it roamed the streets
it escaped the barbed wire the crazy hare
it would fall in mud

Daybreak glowed the crazy hare
the night opened
hearts dripped blood the crazy hare
the world shone

Its eyes brimmed with tears the crazy hare
its tongue swelled
a black insect moaned the crazy hare
death in its mouth

The Soldier Poet

I have not written poems
amid alarms
amid alarms
has my life gone its way

One day I tremble
the next day I shudder
in fear
in fear
has my life moved on

I have not written poems
I have not written poems
I only nail
crosses
on graves

Life

Night
in a pharmacy
a kneeling
horse
eats
the floorboards
a girl
with a strange
green
burn
is being healed
while
the ghost
in despair
weeps
in the corner

The Garden

It smelled of fever
this wasn't a garden
certain strange couples went walking there
wearing shoes on their *hands*
their feet were large white and bare
with heads like wild epileptic moons
and red roses suddenly
sprouted
for mouths
on which butterfly-dogs rushed
and tore them to pieces

Winter

How beautifully have the flowers withered
how perfectly have they withered
and this crazy man running in the streets
with the frightened heart of a swallow
it has turned winter and the swallows have gone
the streets have filled with puddles
two black clouds in the sky
look into one another's eyes angrily
tomorrow the rain also will come out into the streets
in despair
distributing her umbrellas
the chestnuts will be jealous of her
and fill up with yellow wrinkles
and the other shopkeepers will come out
he who sells ancient beds
he who sells the warmest fleeces
he who sells scalding salépi*
and he who sells sheaths of cold snow
for impoverished hearts

*A hot drink of Turkish origin made of various
 herbs and a dash of cinnamon, sold by street
 vendors on cold days. [Tr.]

Stranger

Stranger
with your black suit
who knock on my door
and show me these white plates
where have you hidden your pistol
where have you hidden your knife
you have a red star in your head
and you stammer
you want the money
the money that merged with blood and vanished
the money that merged with sleep and vanished
you implore
go
go stranger
I keep a tame bird in my heart
if I set it free
its teeth will tear you to pieces

from THE STROLL (1960)

Autumn

What is the girl seeking
in the darkness of the chair?
Quickly
as autumn falls into night
she undresses
with clouds before her eyes
with rain inside her head
with a needle in her heart
she takes off her stockings
takes off her flowers
throws away her halo

outside the leaves of time
are dyed in blood

The Story of a Child

To E.H. Gonatás

For years
the sky
was a difficult piece of paper
hidden
in my pocket
and blood
grew in my garden all day long
because stones
fell in rain from the other sky
crushing
meat
and bones

And so when the Resurrection came
I dressed in black
and with a red candle
went out
into the streets
insane

I was a yellow bird
like those Modigliani
drew
I had never
I had never
been born

Thoughts

Quiet coffins of sleep
beds of dreadful death
after he had roamed around the wind of this earth
the wind bolted and bit
the earth turned upside down
from that side where things blossomed
he paused then
thoughtfully
multicolored
near the sea
like a scarecrow on the beach

Pentagram

Limned mouths
the fire entered
the smoke
smashed your teeth

a girl
burned her dress
because she was freezing
she says: I love frozen garments
and I hold only one flower for you
thank you

a beggar
says: Do you know what?
a father has become
a pistol
but I
have a large room
with red curtains
go away!
you are not men
you are moons
I never want to see you again!

a man
searches
the streets
picks up pieces
of paper
cigarette boxes
smiles
and says: I am a murderer
what else?

and I
heavy of heart
annihilated
in difficult times
together with these
burst in a white death
with blood

Why

Why did the blood of winter
sprout wings in spring
and fly in summer?
why did the flowers I planted in my garden
grow wild in my bedroom mirror?
why did the beautiful white body I held
grow black
and dye my hands?
why do birds measure the spring with knives?
why did the diseases of summer
appear in the winter's moon?
why did the black hair I wound around my hands
become spiders and dirty leather?
why did my coffee cup
fill with a dark green martyrdom?

There is no red answer
as to why a large lack
is something like a grave

The Morning and the Evening

In the morning
you see death
gazing from the window
at the garden
at the cruel bird
and the quiet cat
on the branch

outside on the road
the automobile ghost
the hypothetical chauffeur
the man with the broom
and the golden teeth
pass by
he laughs
and in the evening
at the movies
you see
whatever you did not see in the morning
the joyful gardener
the real automobile
the kisses with a real couple

you see that the movies
do not love death

The Station

In memory of Guillaume Apollinaire

In my sleep it is always raining
my dream fills with mud
there is a dark landscape
and I am waiting for a train
the station-master gathers daisies
that have sprouted amid the rails
because no train has come
to this station for a long time
and the years have suddenly passed
I sit behind a windowpane
my hair and beard have grown long
as though I were very ill
and as sleep takes me once more
she comes slowly slowly
she holds a knife in her hands
she approaches me carefully
and plunges it in my right eye

The Money

To Tatiána Milliex

The gypsy woman says:
I read money
in your sleep
you have a crowded life
filled with snow
but I do not know
when
you will slide on

the shepherd says:
When you do not love the stars
my sheep will hate you
and I shall give you
that half of the moon
which vomits flame
from the side of rage

death says:
The money is mine
the moon also is mine
the snow and the sheep are mine
and the red flame
and
the gypsy woman
and
the shepherd

The Nobleman

I shall light up the dark savage palace blindingly
I shall cast colors everywhere
in a dark corner
the d r a g o n
shall be
the branch
of a blossomed
almond tree

because this year in truth I feared
the frost the loneliness the cold
and these deer that passed suspiciously
at night
under my soul

One Day

Blear-eyed are the eyelashes of day
a girl hangs over the windowsill like a flower
though around her the birds are passionately singing
a shattered water glass
with its splinters invisible in the heart
and a paper kite high up like a rebellious dream
emits flame
we gather needles
as in another time they gathered flowers
and the largest pierce
right through our skulls

The Clock

Black is the sun
in my mother's
garden
with a tall green
top hat
my father
would bewitch the birds
and I
with a deaf
and distrustful clock
count the years
and
wait for my parents

from THE STIGMATA (1962)

The Mirror

When my mirror had returned
to the sky
a moon half-eaten
by the red ants of fire
appeared
with a head beside it
also burning in a fiery rain
the head glittered
and glowed
and whispered
as the fire took it and turned it to coal:
The trees burn and disappear like hair
the angel vanishes with scorched wings
and pain
a dog with a broken leg
remains
remains

Moments

the lover
a sick fish
at any moment now
will fall
into the sky
*

I never expected
a hell
with so much light
turning the corner
to confront
the black red
*

locked up
at night
in cages of rain
I am slowly slowly
killed
by birds
*

and in the morning
if the birds
sent me by God
are black again
I shall dye them
green
yellow
red
but one day
the everlasting clouds
will come
*

cypress tree
red
skin
of the soul
          *

A sweet hand
broken
cast
on stones
on the street
on chaos
          *

goodnight

Episode

With the voracious cotton
of death

A large hole opens
in the moon

A child dies

A funeral procession in the moon
like large black ants

Another child
casts a stone
and breaks the moon

I Win

Each day
a black veil falls
and is burnt in the sun
at night
the moon stains it with blood
every night I win I win
my death
stretches out its hand
each night I win I win

The Sun One Beautiful Day

It was a beautiful corner
a beautiful day
creaking and burning with subterranean sound
the sun would rise deeply
and then vanish strangely
there was a beautiful corner
a beautiful day
butterflies would fly
into my death
and the sun would suddenly rise
and afterwards
would vanish extinguished
forever

Clepsydra

All things round her
now
are warm
only at times

she remembers

she felt cold then
rain was falling
and in the darkness
the stranger soldier
with the cigarette
was suspiciously
lurking

—But You God
have forgotten me
the birds
found
only my imprinted
red
shape
on the wall

Sunset

To Aléxi Fasianós

This sudden frost
in the midst of summer

the eyes of my girl
grow glazed
she says: I am spotted
all over
with red evil
but as clean
as a fawn
what shall I do
far from the wellspring?

the other man passes
in gloom
with irons
and a helmet
phosphorizing
locked up
toothless
in a cage
how can he live?

and outside
the sunset
the sounds of animals
lower and dwindle away
pigeons fly upside down
on a forgotten sea
fishes trees flowers
and caïques
drift by sweetly

Portrait

His head
in a gold circle

snow falls upon it

his mouth emits fiery
wounds

wild anemones pursue him

an azure rod stretches above him

about him fly the small black crosses of spring
the swallows

The Desolate

Desolate men in the cold
speak to the Virgin

without expression
without leaves
the trees stare at them

ravens have dressed in red
like whores

the church has cracked
from too much rain
the saints were found
running in the streets

The Poet

When they find me on the wooden slab of my death
the sky will have turned red from end to end
there will be the slightest suspicion of sea
and a white bird from above in a now
frightening darkness will recite my songs

The Gravebird Was Leaving

The gravebird was leaving
so small
mournfully red
and vanished
tenderly
above the sparse grass
with the eternal turtle that trudges silently
the dead locust
and the honeybee
that had wedged itself
painfully
into the flower's mouth

The Gold

One day
we shall stop
like a skyblue coach
in the midst of gold

we shall not count the black horses
we shall have nothing to add
we shall no longer have anything
to share

holding
a stick
we shall pass through the black burning hole
of the sun

Parable

(the metaphysical night or the snow)

The black crow
returns from its trip
with its black overcoat
its black shoes
its black cane

it shakes off the snow

a star has gone into its right eye

the star casts a dreadful radiance
in the radiance the tear
of the other man grows larger
the clamor is dazzling

it kills   it does not blind

the red mouth blows
a tattered rag of black snow

Clean Monday
February 25, 1963

Threnody

Girls like torn cardboard
with stains of sulphur in their heads
with angry weeds in their mouths
smashing the cup of the sky
with tears straining in their eyes
like black brand-new pins
when will the color of birds sing?
when will butterflies strike at knives?
When other hands sprout on suns
and sleep drains them of darkness

and night shall be as beautiful as day

Papers

Gathering
papers
our doves
we shall leave tonight

it will be a lovely trip
the sky
will keep turning a stone on high
pretending to be the sun
the dogs will bark behind it
we shall give our two black hands
we shall clasp our two hands so tightly
they will never be able to part

and the sun will fall headlong
and crush them

Hook

He squeezes his rotted hair
sprouts wings
the girl begins to fly

the telephone howls in the sky
the snow casts down
pieces of white angels

the red girl
is seized by the rain
and hidden in the moon's deep wound

the girl open
glittering

like a black hand whispers
my name

Sunday

My eyes are Sunday waves
my hands are waves of loneliness

the teeth in my heart
grind in an innocent sleep

the dead child
does not live abroad
it walks on holding a small red dog
in a handkerchief

monsters walk
upside down in dreams
a fierce wind is blowing
above the lemonades

a bat flies
like a sorrowful gospel

with a black cloth
a woman covers
the moon

Benjamin

When Benjamin awoke and heard
the birds warbling
We also—he said—had a caged bird
let's go now to see what's become of it.
He went and the cage was a black cup
in which a small goldfish was burning
It's still flaming—he said—we thought it had burned
    down
many years ago.

The Huge Moon

Flooded by the blood of birds
the moon remains hidden
sometimes behind trees
sometimes behind beasts
sometimes behind clouds
with a noise that deafens the wings of angels
they want to say something, they want to hint at something
it is still summer
but a sulphurous smell walls up the winter
there isn't even a chair to sit on
and the chairs have left for the sky

We See with Teeth

The moon is not to blame for our bitterness
as it whirls demoniacally in the phosphorescence
scattering its bones to right and left
as we too whirl in our darkness
scattering our bones to right and left
the moon is not to blame for lemon flowers
the moon is not to blame for swallows
the moon is not to blame for Spring and crosses
it is not to blame if teeth have sprouted out of our eyes

The Canary

They erected him high where the wildest wind blows
they assigned him to the frosts
they gave him a black suit
and a red tie
a dripping sun pierced by a nail
black glasses
blood on poison
a spear
and a canary
they raised him high where pain writhes
they gave him to death
that he might shine in silver

from THE VESSEL (1971)

The Carriage

I went away, my eyes wrapped up in rags
and tore the cloth
my mouth a sewn wound
and I tore my mouth
March threw drops of ice in my eyes and
my eyes turned red
I saw the black glass
steaming no
it wasn't the glass
but a black girl shining
with her hands and head thrown over
as upside down she leant
in chaos smiling at the blue
and falling

I had no luck

Give me a bit of bed, Sky
my house has caught on fire
it rolls it rolls creaking
like a wounded carriage

The Color of Ice

Is the color of rain
white?
green?
or is it perhaps blue?

one studies a peach
the other studies a cross
another the fire of a cross
and another the frozen shadow of a cross

at times a tear grows large
like a round balloon
that ascends together with the cross
and the fire burns it and tears it down

in the frozen shadow of a cross
its fire sits
drinks the tear that falls from the cross
and trembles

a bird somewhere sings
a moon ascends without body
while the body decays far away

come, let's forget
I my drowned flower
you the ice that hunts you down

The Collector

I collect stones stamps
medicine caps broken glasses
corpses from the sky
flowers
and whatever in this savage world
is good
and is endangered

I watch the Bearded Vulture dwindling away
like a paper kite on high

I touch electric wires fearlessly
they do not touch me

the sun gathers up my days
laughing

only my soul whispers
in my ear saying:
it's grown dark it's grown dark
why?
aren't you frightened?

It's Not by Chance that I Live Further On

It's not by chance that I live further on

It darkens from the other side as I watch
the white houses and the black houses
what marked hand will touch me now?
demonic red wheels are always rolling
from a swarm of children
a death nests in each of their bodies
they have turned it into a joyful hoop
and hit it with a small stick
the hoop rolls and rolls, they roll it
their life rolls, a sun that chills them
as with the stick they hit
the frozen death that runs

around them mourning stiffens into speechlessness

it's not by chance that I live further on

Sparrows

Happy those moments
when warm sparrows
flit through the brain
when lips grow large and warm
we win ideal lotteries in the blood
and cigarettes emit a red smoke
and hair grows as long as legends

what a rare sight in atrocious times
when even the dolls of small children
grow black with terror

The Poet's Head

I cut off my head
put it on a plate
and took it to my doctor

There's nothing wrong with it, he told me
it's simply incandescent
throw it into the river and we shall see

I threw it into the river with the frogs
It was then it set all bedlam loose
It began to sing some strange songs
to grate dreadfully and to howl

I took it and wore it again on my neck

I roamed the streets in rage

with the green hexagonometric head of a poet

Heavenly Reply

When I voyaged in the Heavens
I never once met the astronaut
but I met God
with his colored angels

The astronauts are always paid
but God is never paid
nor his colored angels

and when I too send my crafty collector

he always returns empty-handed.

The Enigmas

These black spring flowers
they've planted in my head
are not *crypts*
they are *cryptograms*
whose predictions
I was not able to decipher
when they came
and so into my body now they cast
their definitive inks
they sketch me with their arteries
like certain multicolored advertisements
of foreign pharmaceutical companies
PFIZER'S or GEIGY'S
or ABBOTT'S or BAYER'S

The Green Afternoon

On that green afternoon
death had set my front yard for his target
from my dead window
with my velvet eye
I watched him prowling
he wandered about pretending to be a seller of buns
he wandered about pretending to be a lottery vendor
and the children suspected nothing
they played with pistols and shrieked
and he'd wander about again and approach
then retreat again and go away
afterwards he'd come back
finally he fell into a rage
and began to howl
he painted his eyes and his nails
swelled out his dugs
began to speak in a falsetto voice
acted like a woman . . .

it was then he went away for good
whispering:

—I've had no luck today
tomorrow I'll be back

The Coffee House

I was sitting in the coffee house looking out the window
a woman without hands was trying
to hide a telephone in her mouth
that fat red bird that always pursues me
flew round about me three times
afterwards stood by the entrance of the coffee house
and shouted to me:
You're naive, you don't know anything, I shall kill you!
Then I set myself to singing
about the white woman made of sugar who died with the nuns

everything was so ugly so horrible
that I began to laugh
to laugh
to laugh

I saw myself also passing by outside the window

he was infinitely sad and thoughtful

Sir

To Kiriákos Rókos

—Sir, it's midday and you've not yet wakened
—Sir, you've not had your breakfast
—Sir, you've drunk many cups of coffee
—Sir, it's flashing, it's raining, it's snowing, the sun is shining
—Sir, a red bird has glued itself to your window
—Sir, a black butterfly has appeared on your chest
—Sir, how fast you're speeding on your bicycle!
—Sir, you're frozen
—Sir, you've a fever

—Sir, are you dead?

The Ascent

The poet whirls round and round on his wheel
the poet whirls round and round demoniacally
the head of a horse smashed on his feet
a woman opens her white mouth to bite
poisonous snakes encircle him
coins roll on the ground
cracked skulls are cast in his mud
and round steel flowers are whistling

as the poet whirls round and round
he begins to ascend
as he turns in frenzy
as he turns frenetically
he begins to ascend

one of his hands has stopped burning
the other is holding a flaming coal

To the End

On the mattress his body passed through terrifying phases. One
of his feet became as thin as a thread and the other as thick
as a tree trunk.
He felt however that his fist had become dreadful and as his
bed was against the wall he wanted with one blow to pierce the
wall until his hand passed through into the adjacent apartment.
Many times as he was walking on the street he suddenly felt
his entire body becoming so incandescent that it might suddenly
shoot upward like a bullet.
(And this he wanted exceedingly)
But he sat quietly in the coffee house playing with his worry
beads, drinking his coffee . . .
He thought his name was Dzáko or Dzakópoulo or something of
the sort.

from COLOR WOUNDS (1980)

The Letters

I shall stop writing poems
you cast your golden ring into the sea
on the sand with the dead skull
and all the sunken ships emerged upon the foam
and the captain living
and the crew smiling

I said I shall stop writing poems now

and at the window of my ancestral home
my father and my mother
wave their handkerchiefs in greeting

but they cannot read my poems
they've forgotten how to read
they call the *k* an *a* and the *d* an *e*
and you lied to me
in this land of the red laughing skull you deceived me
and so I deceived you also
and you believed me

may you be cursed with the seven shadows

I shall always write poems

The Hands the Record of Love

Soldiers still return from battles
        they lost
Soldiers still return from battles
        they won

      they turn
      like a record

they gather dreams on street corners
and set them on fire

hairs still hang and suns that have turned white
fall one creaking after the other
moons suddenly are pierced even from the inside
(moons—I said—not carcasses)
. . . and heads emerge from inside
ah, yes, your head, my love
I've not seen it for many years
ah, yes, the moon, my love
I've not held its hand for many years

now moons do not have two
they do not have five a hundred
a thousand hands

my love has gone
with the tired soldiers
the suns
the moons

needle-heart
how can it play a record

broken
broken
broken

a thousand years ago

The English Poet and Painter
Dante Gabriel Rossetti
Writes a Poem with my Hand

Listen!
I told you the truth then
I knew the truth then

—No, you'd say to me
birds sprout
pigs fly
flowers walk
men always tell lies

I'd show you a bird
you'd say—It's a flower
I'd show you a flower
no, you'd say—It's a bird

and men always tell lies

Now I look at the moon
this broken spastic
child
about which
Jules Verne
once said:
—Men will inhabit it

I see
that large snow-covered coffin
on which they throw nails every day
with a loud noise
and insist
on naming it

EARTH

perhaps you were right then

this is why you could live
this is why I could live

DAWN

The Radiance

—Do you fly, the one who held the knife asked him.
The other very slowly no longer stepped on the ground, very
    slowly
had risen about half a meter above the earth.
—And yet—said the first:
I can even as you are rising
stab you with the knife.
And then the other with a radiance
and a deafening whistle like a bullet from a machine gun
vanished, disappeared in the distance.

The one who remained looked with astonishment
at his now useless hand.

The Violet

Tak-tak
a young man's step
douk-douk
an old man's step

into the coffee house
steps Mr. Hermes
with his ten canes

and orders:

—Eleven coffees

one for himself
one for each of his canes

what short violet
is life . . .

and I who had planned
to wander to wander
throughout all of P a r a d i s e !

Ectoplasms

In my grave
I walk in agitation
up and down
up and down

I hear things around me howling
ideas-automobiles
automobiles-ideas

Men pass by
they speak, they laugh
for me

they tell truths
they tell lies
for me, for me!

—Don't, I shout to them
don't speak
about my dead loves

they will waken
they will gouge out your eyes!

Asái*

When you were ascending the mountain
you were descending to the plain
to hunt souls
to chase white butterflies
and you thread them on thin silver wires
for you are the same person ascending
and the one descending
the butterfly then is not the butterfly
the dead woman is not the dead woman
nor is the grave her grave
— Asái, I shouted to you therefore
as I spoke to you, descending the stairs
I the same person ascending
and we almost crashed into one another
I proceeding toward the Heavens
I falling headlong
both of us shouting:

— Asái   Ezmé**   Ezmé   Asái

*A fictitious name or sound. [Tr.]
**A Turkish name for a girl. [Tr.]

Míltos Sahtoúris was born in Athens in 1919, though he considers Hýdra, the island of his ancestors, as his place of origin. He has devoted his life exclusively to poetry and has published ten books of poems since 1945. While confining himself mostly to one neighborhood in Athens, he has created a poetry of images which vividly reflects the dislocations of the contemporary world. Once markedly surrealist, his poetry has become increasingly lyrical and dramatic, and the gaping wounds which his poems reveal float in a metamorphosis of color. The poetic space which he creates has affinities with the imagery of painters such as Bosch and Chagall.

Kimon Friar, the eminent translator, poet, scholar and critic, was born of Greek parentage on an island in the Sea of Marmara. He achieved renown as the translator of Nikos Kazantzakis' *The Odyssey, A Modern Sequel.* His anthology, *Modern Greek Poetry* appeared in 1973 and he has published numerous other translations, including works of Odysseus Elýtis and Yánnis Rítsos. He has held several academic positions in the United States and has lectured widely in Europe and the Middle East. He is now at work on anthologies of more recent Greek poets.